THE TASTE OF CYANIDE

AJA

ISBN 979-888521961-7

TO EVERY TEENAGER, WHO WANTS TO QUESTIONS
EVERYTHING.

Contents

1. Shorn Underneath — 1

2. Emotionless — 3

3. The Hungry Dame — 5

4. Midnight Paradise — 7

5. Distress Of Surrender — 8

6. My Two Worlds — 9

7. Uncontrolled Ecstacy — 10

8. River Of Thoughts — 13

9. Everyone Can Lie — 14

10. Rampage — 17

11. Known Monsters — 19

12. A Dull Monotonous Game — 21

13. The Taste Of Cyanide — 22

14. Never Reaching........ — 24

15. The Sound Of My Pen — 26

16. This Is Me — 28

17. Share Of Mock — 29

18. A Bit Of You — 30

19. The Woman — 31

20. Maybe It's..... — 32

21. Tired Of Society — 33

22. Karma — 35

23. Dark Moments — 37

24. Toxic Love — 39

Contents

25. On The Falling Edge 41

26. The Magical Rose 43

27. Demon 44

28. The Untitled Feelings 45

29. Who Will Find Me? 47

30. Just A Prisoner 49

31. My Imaginery Friend 51

32. A Letter To The Lost 53

33. My Sleeping Paralysis 54

34. A Broken Freedom 55

35. Time Flies 56

36. Numb 57

37. Love And Cigaretts 58

38. A Tremandou Dynamism 59

39. Irreplacable Void 60

40. Something Must Be 61

41. Dystopia 62

42. Bueaty Hurts 63

43. Peak Of Mind:first Side 64

44. Peak Of Mind: Other Side 65

1. SHORN UNDERNEATH

New chapter, same line
New beginnings, same sunshine.
Tomorrow upholds mysteries
But we choose to repeat yesterday's miseries
Imprisoned in nostàlgic memories
Clutched to the strings of the past
Trampling on mines just to burst
Not a step backward nor forward
Just swallowed by a quicksand
Trapped b/n fear and despair
Overwhelmed by blighted hope
Little by little there goes the flare
Worn out from the slippery slope

Frozen in doubts of a fallacy
For me or for you should I be sorry
For your assumptions or for believing your story
Should I frown cause the truth is blurry
All the murmuring fingers pointed at me
Things aren't like they're meant to be
My efforts are all seen merely

Invisible in crowds
As my thought to silence bows
Too drained too feel
Too fragile to heal
To apathetic to appeal
I don't know where to find the switch kill
This days beside attention what do we seek
Maybe a little love a little hope a little empathy
Yeah the things that labels us weak
Building up a wall not to be taken as pity
Maybe we're different yet similar after all
Trying to fill a trench we dig up a hole
As one foot escapes the other fell
Hidden in smirks to eachother we're hell
I just wonder if we all are hurt at once
Maybe we'll bleed but our hearts won't be at distance
Maybe we'll laugh cry and dance
But our hell would be heaven that brings us closer
For we would feel the painful wounds together

2. EMOTIONLESS

When I pray,
God doesn't listen
though I am sad,
God doesn't listen
but
mesmerizing smile
of peach blossoms,
scintillating joy
of maple trees,
asking me
the reason of my anguish?
I am stuck
in the thoughts
of past hurdles,
unable to move
and a river flowing
through the bends,
asking me why can't
you get across?

Am I emotional or
Are they emotionless?
one day everything's going

to fade out, buried under soil

the eyes of the Dog,
the feather of the bird
asking me
Why are you emotional ?
why can't you be like us ?

3. THE HUNGRY DAME

She comes at the street, takes a heavy rest; beside the

Newborn grass rounded-leaves with a soft stick, giggly circle;

Stones there and in mind of the Dame. Someone calling the

Lady's kins near the house of her; heavy rest, all see her;

Looking panic-rage mouth, elbows on her knees; married

Twice, eloped; Adeline claims WHY? she here -

Everyone sees her by frightening-muddle eyes, she opens her jib:

She came to the office for importance, but the mouth

In too hungry, for relatives and food. So disappears

From her husband's house and office, direct way to

Her father's house. Belongs to roadside not dare

To admit her misdeed to the House. For:

She'd already deeded two fallacies to her family.

Her eyes deep into and make it black both in up

And down; like a place where forward and

Backward with death. Possibly once a day

BLACK ups and downs match her eyes to close.

She's hungry for her husband's house, suffer

Here's eat by a seven-days. She just comes here

To fill her tummy full of food and water.

Just want to fill! but fail both in the houses.
The Hungry Dame just wants to fill with
Food and water and to live, heavenly bliss.

• 6 •

4. MIDNIGHT PARADISE

I was out on the terrace in the dead of night talking to the moon

Secrets that glow in the dark, the one's the light wouldn't approve

I showed my bare skin on which the years wrote their eminence

I slid off the clothes that suffocated me under the moon's candescence

I wasn't obliged to hide my twisted feelings behind a lady's courtesy

Now is when they show their colors and dance blithely

There are no forbidden deeds nor off-limit places

I and my demons dance until We are exhausted

Till its dawn and I return to the prosaic life

I'll dance to the owl's tune, cheating the light.

5. DISTRESS OF SURRENDER

She has fought several wars before this,
But this is a fight everyone will reminisce
Her wings replace the ammunition in this fight,
But she still soars above the populace with all her might
For this fight may take away her bag of bones,
But her ardor is more ferocious than the worst of cyclones
For this fight may take away the affirmation,
It cannot crumble her affection
For this fight may damage her control,
It will never cripple her soul
For this fight may leave her incapable,
It cannot leave her in shambles,
This courage, she has, it's not meant to holler,
It keeps quiet and grows silently in her heart's corner
For this fight might try its best to pull her down,
To the deep dark dungeons underground
To cuff her hands with the strongest of chains,
And gag her with the clothes as rusty as a crane
But she will still fight to survive,
And she will rise beyond the archetype
Because she is an angel with wings so high and sleek,
This cancer will be the one to face defeat.

6. MY TWO WORLDS

There is a tiny world inside this wide big world,

That doesn't exist but is very real.

It has noise.

It has a pleasant voice.

It has pain.

It is complete and very serene,

Just like the world outside of it.

In this little world,

I can be as crazy as I want.

As wise as possible,

With nobody noticing it.

I have faced many challenges here,

Sunk in too many hardships.

Still, I call it my safest place,

My home, sweet home!

This bit is all that I know,

And that's how I know the world outside of it.

7. UNCONTROLLED ECSTACY

Through the crumbling ruins and holy shrines of the
memories ,
lost in sands of time ,
that midnight invites
into my every single,
private thought ,
the picture of you rushing ,
flooding
my combined synapses
in a brilliant
rush of uncontrolled ecstasy longing...
the emotions running
from nowhere
to everywhere ,
hurting and caressing
every nerve in the body
that mellows and forms
under your every touch.
I'm drunk ,
for that I truly do apologize.
I am sober
yet so incredibly

intoxicated
by every abstractable
essence of the beautiful angel
I have dared to love ,
to hold ,
to kiss.
The very thought
of you
makes me want to
scream and cry ,
to laugh and love ,
to live and die.
I'm a runaway horse
running on a train track ,
an omega wolf
seeking every star
in order to find you...
I'm a writer of words
that flows from inside
to every piece of white
that might care
to sacrifice
everything
that might leave me hanging
between the moon and sun , right between the rivers and seas
,
lost on both heaven and earth.

It's a neverending fountain
from inside my soul ,
my heart that echoes ,
" I love you! "
as though it was bottled up
for centuries ,
ages , eons.

8. RIVER OF THOUGHTS

There is a World too much within Us,

Forever in a Mood to follow a Profane Rush.

The Mind, Body and the Soul emerge into an endless Fight,

Meanwhile the one who suffers the rage,seems to be my Appetite.

My Mind is like a River of Thoughts,

Searching for an Ocean, before they turn into Knots.

For the Soul never agrees to that of Mind,

Now the battle has turned into another Kind.

When the Body at the end is Left to Decide,

The Mind doesn't like to join the Ride.

All of them wants to be set Free,

For the Chaos has Arisen between these three.

Who is the superior of them all?

The world decides after making each one fall.

Now as I begin to listen to my Soul,

The other two are Satisfied as they reach their Goal.

9. EVERYONE CAN LIE

From the young to the old.

From those who are not that bold,

And shiver to speak as if with cold.

To those who talk without fear,

And those who shed all sorts of crocodile tears.

Don't be deceived, everyone can lie.

From those who claim to love,

Yet cannot even sacrifice what they have.

From those with innocent looks.

To the annoying ones with weird looks.

From those as fat as an inflated balloon,

To those as slim as the half moon.

From the gentle jacks who stand tall,

To those who crawl or don't walk at all.

Even those behind the pulpit,

Narrate the scriptures into fibs,

False doctrines being bathed on their culprits.

Yet they still bless with their holy lips.

Don't be deceived, everyone can lie.

From those who are married,

To those who are single and unmarried.

Everyone lies about one thing or another,

Just to impress or maintain the other.

To those who are in power,

And those seeking it however.

Present lies through propaganda notes,

Just to secure some electoral votes.

So don't be deceived, everyone can lie

For those who are hungry,

Manipulate lies to be filled.

And those who are filled,

Fabricate the truth to get thrilled.

From the beloved and highly favoured,

To the foe and those merely hated.

None can forever be honest,

Especially when put to a solicit test,

For lies is ever accustomed in our society,

And technology has even made it a normality.

So Just ask where have you gotten to,

And the answer will be "I just drove passed the zoo",

Meanwhile, he or she is at home,

Now dressing up and busily looking for comb.

Don't be deceived, everyone can lie.

People hide their right entity,

To impress the inquisitive society,

By presenting false identity.

The truth sometimes seem bitter,

So we perceive the bitters as lies,

And the sweet as truth.
But to my poem alone,
Am sure is not a lie,
That everyone can lie.

10. RAMPAGE

There's a knife stuck in my heart
My body's marred with scars
The pain is unbearable
The bleeding isn't light
You've wrecked me with all
Your ignorance and lies
Yet I take it all and give us a chance
No need to say things
To multiply the distance
A stake embedded in my soul
A poison avoiding me to grow
A gag avoiding me to shout
A shackle holding me down
There's so much I wanna pour out
Maybe these trapped emotions
These deadly confined feelings
Will run loose one day
Maybe I'll bite back
Maybe I'll retort
Maybe ur pouring gasoline
Maybe one day ill combust
Maybe it'll all crumble down
Maybe I'll fall out of sort

What comes up will sure fall
Maybe I'll stop being your doll
And throw up all you fed me
Venom coated with ecstasy
One day I might unlock the cage
Set my fury up in a rampage.

11. KNOWN MONSTERS

You love her,
But you don't confess.
You are impaired,
Yet you hold your tears.
You are insecure,
Which is clear from that messy mind.
You are irascible,
Yet you control it.
You start concealing;
Your hurricane inside you.
And slowly and steadily,
A monster starts prevailing beneath you.
Your blood boils at high temperature.
You are stressed at any tenure.
The pain which you felt,
Has been a chunk of life now;
And the tears which wanted to flow,
Had now decided to stay inside.
Silence....
Your monster loves this silence.
Your monster makes your heart lose feelings.
Your monster builds walls around your heart;

And make you cold, full of venom.
But my dear,
Hear to the jingling bells,
Your life is calling you.
Don't miss that call;
And don't let that monster to germinate inside you.
Unfurl yourself;
Clear up your messy mind.
Uproot the seeds,
That let the devil develop beneath you.

12. A DULL MONOTONOUS GAME

Slowly time melts;

Teasingly slow, tantalizingly lazy, dripping from above in slow measured drops...

Time is just crawling;

In a dull monotonous game, scraping through just inches...

Time has just about reached the point of slow march;

Its legs are strong enough to hold step after step, but still staggeringly slow, sloppily sloths...

Time is now like a drugged bee;

roaming around in circles, gathering momentum and desperate to make a leap and fly...

Oh, time!!!

Time has flown…

Like a stream of jet water, that has attained nirvana...

Free from the hindering bonds of slowness...

Time jumping in joy, flipping in the air, heading to the sky;

faster and faster like the rearing waves, faster than lightning...

Not anymore, can it be held?

13. THE TASTE OF CYANIDE

You made me fall in love with my pain and suicide
Nowadays I basically die every night
because every moment we spend away is cyanide
I'm enslaved by the way you captivate my mind
You drive me crazy in your blue Pontiac Vibe
In its backseat, I lose myself between your thighs
Then I say 'I love you but you know it's a lie
Cz my actions, love can't even begin to describe
I wanna scream from the rooftops that you're mine
I wanna go to heaven and tell God I've found paradise
I've found the girl who can teach the sun how to shine
I've found the one flame that sets my world alight
Tell him I've found my apple slice
Show him that I've already taken a bite
And now my mind has come alive
I never wanted to fall yet I spiral within your eyes
You see right through my deceptions and lies
Strip me till I'm vulnerable and shy
Then watch my pain masquerade as pride
You're the only one who sees the Nii I'm tryna hide
I can't seem to lie to you no matter how hard I try
If love was a drug, then you are my prescription

You're always on my mind, you're my addiction

Your love gets me high

Till I float above cloud nine

Till I walk on stardust and dine on sunshine

So I guess then it's time

The world needs to know that this coach about to play this game.

14. NEVER REACHING........

I always failed

Being human is weakness by itself

Grace became too hard for me to claim

My sins, too hard for me to face.

Being a better person isn't as easy as they say

The light is flower-covered with thorns

And Whetted leaves

Surrounded by cutting grass

Growing on soil filled with broken glass

I see at last my salvation

Only to know I could never reach it.

Please,

Understand the weakness that is a part of me as much as are

the cells in my body

Claiming that I'm stronger wouldn't make me one

So I won't dare lie.

Please,

I'm not saying it's too much

Just that I'm to frail to handle it

I know no good deed goes unpunished

I know I must bleed but show me how not to bleed too much

Let me feel a study heartbeat so I don't pace
Tell me that I am not my mistakes
That although my sins can't be erased they can be forgiven
That I have underestimated my strength
That my chance of deliverance didn't quite fade
Show me that I'm not all body and no soul
That I'm not too monster to tame
Show me....the gates of heaven aren't that far away.

15. THE SOUND OF MY PEN

I wrote

A wish for an adventure, I gave myself wings of magic for a doomed journey,

Felt like my life missed a spice, some mythical story to fit the crooks and complete me,

I landed on the most gentle hands, with eyes so pure and a soul-deep as the sea.

I wrote

An honoring piece, for the refuge I found, one that kept me alive,

For the healing touch that caressed my scars, passing every line,

For my long-sought share of joy that finally became mine.

I write

To keep that jewel of memory, the fresh set of pain, springing with life,

To keep an eye on my demons, for them to never find a place to hide,

It's but a necessity that I lift my pen, it's to cage the chaos of my mind.

When I am writing those,

the pen glides gracefully across my paper as though whispering secrets
It took the demons, the chaos, the darkness, and questions out of my heart's chambers
Unto the white parchment, where it'll remain safe and far from anyone's judgment,
far from anyone's ears.

16. THIS IS ME

This is me
Headstrong, with billions of thoughts running in my head
Believe me, I've tried to quieten the noises but I failed
I've befriended some when they came rushing to my aid.
This is me
Skeptic, with billions of scenarios building up every second
All ending up with me a victim in a plot so horrific
Forsaken and betrayed with a broken heart I can never mend.
This is me
Insecure, with billions of flaws, flashing on my eyes
I write about defects and shame on hundreds of pages
But spend days trying to find something good about myself.

17. SHARE OF MOCK

The rueful clues sprung out of the dark
They slithered their way into the thrown larks
All said their share of mock
It gleamed on the faces of the one's she beheld
That she was not what they expected
Speaking of hope and unseen bond
She pranced to the swirl of the wind
Like a flower in the wild
It was not what they wanted
But she still scribbled her thoughts
And they spoke ill of her
Belittling her mind's great invention
She smiled and spilled the beans
Composed colorful melodies
of scars, laughs, healing, and burns
Imperfect and enchanting lives
One that had truth in what could be
One that they couldn't see.

18. A BIT OF YOU

A bit of you might always be scared
A bit of you might always be insecure
A bit of you might always be confused
So you took a back step
Little did you realise
Some bit of you is always confident
Another bit of you is always assertive
And most bit of you always have a vision
Ahh ! While you always doubt for a step ahead
You forget you have wings to fly..Let you be a wild mix of
Immense self trust and wild inhibitions....
Just put on your wings
And fly high and high
Till even sky doesn't seem to be limit...!!!

19. THE WOMAN

•31•

she seems like an old fashioned, dark skinned ,highly adorable
girl...

no, maybe i was wrong she is not the girl anymore i had seen
before,

she is different, no became different

She transformed into a "woman"

the "women" who brought me sunshine,

the "women" who showed me the way of loving oneself ,

the "women" who learns me to worship,

the "women" who cares like a lioness,

she was the "women" who made me a " real "men".

no men is perfect without knowing the way to worship and

respect a women

& a real "women" can only make thier real "men".

20. MAYBE IT'S.....

Maybe what hurts me the most
is the picture in my head
Maybe it's the life
I still wish to have
Maybe it's the mistakes
I always avoid making
Maybe it's the first step
I never try to take
Maybe it's the fears
I created in my mind
Maybe it's the thought
of all what could be mine
Maybe it's the hope
of changing yesterday
Maybe it's the voice inside
that stands in between my way
Maybe it's my lack of reality,
Maybe what hurts me the most is me.

21. TIRED OF SOCIETY

The society is tired of me
And I as well
The politics of eagle-eyed men
The ranting of drooling masses
The wasted saliva of innocents
The society is tired of me
And I as well
The religion of wolf-skinned men
The soiled agbada of ministers
Ministers on seat
Ministers on pulpit
I am tired of Society
Society is tired of me
The gossip that flows with the wind
The market women that flows the gossip
The white house with greened growths
The crooked walls on smooth floors
I am tired of Society
Society is tired of me
Your mother that raises her voice
For fucks that don't matter
You for caring

For fucks that don't matter
Your father that dictates his position
On fucks that don't matter
You for caring and a copycat
The flaws you grabbed
The fucks you gave
The ones you didn't
Tired of Society!

22. KARMA

When you left me in the pit, you said I couldn't fit

To you it was lit, when I became a deadbeat, useless kit

I lost my feet, coz I wasn't fit, to fit

On your sit, or at your feet

You said that's it, and dumped me ten feet,

Now that I'm the hit, you need my pint.

When I was in need, you said we couldn't meet

I had to feed, on the rotten meat and seeds

I had to read, on how to bleed,

In pain without gain,

I lived in a train with stains of pain and strains

Tied with chains of ails, fixed with wrecked nails

Now that I'm the hit, you need my pint

Your success was brief, just like my belief in grief

The lord turned the leaf, and now you are stiff

In just a glimpse, you fell off the cliff

The me you used to tease, is now at peace, taking life at ease,

Now that I'm the hit, you need my pint

I didn't cause your fall, but now its me you call, you had no feelings such a doll,

Your actions I recall, but I will stand tall and take a stroll,

Roll a poll on what to install, against your fall

You treated me ill, but thats not my skill, I gotta drill because

Your dreams I can't kill, instead your spirits i'll refill, and that's my will

Now that I'm the hit, you need my pint

I hope you remember, the last September, that I wasn't a member

In all your tenders

You were busy with that gender, occupied by your own agenda, while I focused on the calendar, with one agenda

To become a leader, and be a winner

Now I'm the heat, and you need my hint.

23. DARK MOMENTS

There are times I'm exhausted and weak
Times I get so down that the sky becomes bleak
Times when my best friend is my ink
And the only thing I do then is just think
I have dark moments
Times when I put on the devil's garment
to pass harsh judgment
and inflict self-torment
Times when I can't care
Times when the light within disappears
And am kept company alone by the night
For them alone knows my plight
Those times, I spend alone
In those times I stay on my own
Lying on my bed restless
Screaming yet voiceless
There are times no one knows about
Times, am full of doubt
Times, my demons shout
And I have no choice but to let them out
But now, those times that are becoming 'Every time'
Seeking relief is such a punishable crime
I have to go about wearing a pretend

Coz those dark moments have refused to END.

24. TOXIC LOVE

In a night all is fine
We on our wine
We talk and all is well
At dawn feelings change
In a second am a stranger
Can someone explain
Whats this we call love
Just a feeling for minites
Or mind games
Am tired of all this
Thats what my mind says
But am still in love
Thats what the heart feels
How do i break free
This dilemma needs a cure
How do you turn nice
In just a snap
Then worse in a blink
How do you even do that
Am parking
Yes am leaving
My heart should sit and watch
As my brain demonstrate

Then this again
How do i leave
That same man
Who happens to be my life
How can i stay away
When i know he is my own.

25. ON THE FALLING EDGE

God's given me a break
A break from the fast lane
Cause I was living without a break
And my mind was racing I was going insane.
I had one night off's
And barely even cared
I was like water on run off's
So fast at speeds I normally never dared.
At one point I was on a cliff
At the very edge
My body was now stiff
Cause I didn't wanna die at this young age.
I cried cause I saw I'm about to fall
And what had taken years
All of it I was about to lose it all
So I came down with tears.
I realized it was all a lie
That I been avoiding the truth
That I was about to die
Yet I've got more to life cause I'm still a youth.
So imma start afresh
Pick up where I left my pieces

And each day I'll write new pieces
To restore the image of me in my mind that's so fresh.

26. THE MAGICAL ROSE

Granny gave me a red rose,

As magical as a genie's lamp

Ice cream was all I could ask for.

I've always had it tucked

Underneath my dark hair,

A tincture of color in my faded cosmos.

At times, the prickles made me bleed

Provoking a desire of abandoning it

But it also alleviated all the miseries of life.

Rose became my intoxicant,

Devoid of lethality,

Could never be alone till I had this home.

Eventually, it lost its scent

And manifested discoloration;

The sky was gloomy as this dusk had no dawn.

I bade goodbye with white roses

On the grave of that red rose.

Now, its petals reside in pages of my book.

My daughter is as delicate as that rose

Dressed in black she asks me,

"An ice cream?"

27. DEMON

Putting the pieces back to life
I stumbled on another piece of a lie.
While drawing the pictures for you,
I witnessed another demon just insight.
A queen or a demon?
You gave me memories of that torment.
To wonder if you're still human,
Is the shame I have to live by.
To change you might not be easy;
Since you're the demon I help create.
I want it to stop so badly
And I'll pierce my heart if ever needed.

28. THE UNTITLED FEELINGS

Was she really broken?
Or a part of her was stolen?!
The scars defined her,
The pain made her.
All the sufferings she could bear,
Was just a path taken devoid of fear.
The pale face has agony
Will there ever be a symphony?
In the forest woods, in the cold desserts
She could find herself breaking bit by bit
Was she really made to fit?
(Every single time)
Still, her lips formed a curve and she smiled
Leaving the dark shadows far away in miles
Whatever she did was really tough
Then why did she feel handcuffed?
To everyone she proved herself to be a pixie dust
But for them..was she just a lust?
No more songs were heard
No more memories made
Because sadness is what was to be laid

She needs no answers because that may scare her more
Deep inside she would feel herself a bit torn.
Will she get up strong?
And will show everyone where she belongs?
She needs to do it all again...
Or else all the sacrifices would go in vain.

29. WHO WILL FIND ME?

I am standing right here
but no one seems to see me
I am speaking
but no one seems to hear me
I am writing this down
but no one seems to read it

In this big world
I am a lost soul
that needs to be found
The one who finds me
will find passion and love
and forever listen to the sound
of my grateful voice saying "You found me"

Time passing by
but I am at the same place;
scared
scared for being forever alone
In this big world, I am so small
No one would ever notice
if I called Heaven and asked

if the Angels could find me
in this huge world
At least, the Angels of God
would have found me
and taken me home

I was standing right here
you were the one who saw me
I spoke
you were the one who listened
I wrote this down
you were the one who read it

You are the only one I can trust
You are the only one that cares
You are the only one I need

You are me
and the person
I found in me
was finally myself.

30. JUST A PRISONER

Just a prisoner of my own thoughts

They hold me captive like closed bars

Secluded,alone, living on Mars

I Breath my own air

Don't let anyone close afraid they'd suffocate

But they don't know

They think that they're the problem

Yet the issues are my own

I spend my time counting stars

They seem to be the only things that don't run out

Always thinking,always in doubt

Wondering how long it'd take the one that came to heal me to

call it quits

to develop claustrophobia and decide the cage they entered

was getting too tight for them to breath

It's just a matter of time

I've learned not to have high hope's so I'm never really broken

when they're gone

....only cracked.

Just a prisoner of my own thoughts

They hold me underwater

Gave me gills for my lungs

They made my home the ocean

I don't let anyone come over afraid they'd drown
But they don't know
They think that they're the problem
Yet the issues are my own
I've grown a little strong
Been trying to find the key to the lock that has my fate on
hold
Before my thoughts become kryptonite and pain is all I know

Before the voices turn loud and barricade my soul
Before they convince me...to call this place my home

31. MY IMAGINERY FRIEND

Who were you?

I remembered like it was a yesterday,

A little someone who dressed in all gray,

Feeling too desperate to play,

And making me feel like a prey.

Just, who were you?

I was too naive to understand,

Too careless when it came to believing,

Too reckless when it came to loving,

Why did I allow you to enter my life?

Now, all you do is hurting me like a knife.

What were you?

Pretty on the outside, gritty on the inside,

Like a fallen angel in disguise,

Like a raging wildfire in my eyes,

Why did I trusted you in the first place?

Now, pain and suffer is all I embrace.

Just, what were you?

Wasn't a princess from a fairy tale,

Neither an Aenaes from a folktale,

A violent killer that exist to impale,

A silent thriller that made me question my own existence.

As I got older,

You became stronger while I felt like a goner,

You followed me everywhere,

As if we were an inseparable pair,

Making our bonds unbreakable,

Because you were living inside me after all these while.

As I became wiser,

I'd come to learn your name,

You were a demon that made my whole purpose of life a shame.

32. A LETTER TO THE LOST

Little raindrops drizzle down the skies,

While teardrops mizzle down my eyes,

Listening to our favorite songs,

And thinking of the times that'd gone wrong.

It was a good start,

But now everything is apart,

Regretting every meaningless argument,

And now my shattering heart is all I can hear.

We promised not to leave each other,

Must always be together,

We said that we would venture into the world together,

Do you still remember?

Little snowflakes blew through the wind,

While mistakes breakthrough my inner mind,

Wishing to myself to pause the memories,

Stoping the pain and rewind our rhapsodies.

Without the old you, it's raging and merciless,

Acting out like we are on a river full of sadness,

It sucks away all my life's happiness,

My heart, barely limping through,

I'm not asking for a lot,

All I need is you..

33. MY SLEEPING PARALYSIS

Nothing feels like the late-night visits from the demons of hell,
Anything could happen within a split second as well,
Blink once, it appears.
Blink twice, it disappears.
Nothing feels like my fate being torn apart,
Feeling like endless weights crushing my heart,
Killing me silently under the beaming moonlight,
As if it's trying to suffocate me with all its might.
Not just about turning my body around and wishing to sleep,
But also, a feeling of an embodies scratching my skin deep,
There's something hidden in my closet,
And he's gesturing to me to creep closer.
Not just about being sleepless or becoming restless the very next day,
But also, it's not worth the fight,
I can't stand the very thought of another useless night.

34. A BROKEN FREEDOM

Forgive me as I keep growing tired of breathing,

Revere me for using my strength when I was bleeding,

The path ahead is unpredictable and cryptic,

Like the broken wings of a bird, useless and pathetic.

Forgive me this life of uninhibited love,

An overindulgence of unexpressed freedom,

Although I still fear of being abandoned and forgotten,

It is impossible to neglect the sorrow I've gotten all those years,

But under the vast sky, we shall defend our rights from the shears.

Many times I've faced cold shoulders and ridicule,

Never have I given up my heart's hopes and desires,

Break through this dark prison, a fight to conspire,

Across the boundless sea, let our mind sleep in peace,

An endless cease of the dream that we shall rise for independence.

35. TIME FLIES

Like the little girl, I was, learning to be proud and strong,
Growing up to be a perfect someone who does no wrong,
Head filled with sad songs, not knowing where do I belong,
False hopes and dreams of the future bottled me up all night long.
Time flowed like stars, feet soon decorated with scars,
Heartfelt confidence, unlimited freedom on oneself,
I used to be a child of high expectations on myself,
Now everything has changed before I even knew,
As stared back at the mirror and questioned, "Who are you?"
Hours turned to years have passed and it was a mess,
An endless of greed and ambition increased to impress,
And the friends I had drifted apart one by one,
Lonely without the loved ones, ecstasy was close to none,
I closed my teary eyes to the present that couldn't be altered,
But that was alright, just live life to the fullest, and that was all that ever mattered.

36. NUMB

Time has passed,

Like the smoke particles in the air,

Chaotic silence and painful grief that I'd to bear,

A demanding wish to forget the past,

And the memories of regrets that ripped me apart.

Time has passed,

Like the season of monsoon in a desert,

Feeling like dirt as I embraced my body in hurt,

Nothing to stare at, pure sadness and empty rooms,

My eyes transfixed to an unknown distant,

An endless void, forcing my mind to feel paranoid.

Time has passed,

As the pain and anger numbed me over the years,

Never leaving me like the salt in the sea,

So I welcomed them with open arms,

An unbreakable bond as they became a part of my charms.

"Feelings are what help us grow. They're also what help us connect to people but the existence of numbness I will be there to break that connection."

37. LOVE AND CIGARETTS

Under the galactic sky of thousand stars,

Accompanied by silence and empty streets,

I was alone, a painful feeling of bittersweet,

Pair of drenched eyes and a bleeding heart,

As my mind brought me back to the start,

So I sat down on the pavement and took a deep breath,

Cigarette's end between lips, a tired escape,

The smell of smoke and a bitter taste of death,

Feeling alive inside, as the drugs made me forget my own name,

Quiet ashes fell slowly, like the memories we used to share.

Sad songs and fading colors,

Remembering memories from last summer,

The relationship was like an ocean and you were my deep sea,

So I used cigarettes and burning flames every day,

To extinguish the feeling of drowning alone,

A relief, watching the clouds filled with regrets escaped as I blow.

One was never enough,

Like coffee, I became addicted because of you.

38. A TREMANDOU DYNAMISM

I drift in and out of people's lives,

Like an elegant crane in the winter season,

So it won't be a surprise,

If I leave everyone in the dust without a reason.

I hate making myself comfortable,

As if I'm at home having cookies and a cup of tea,

It Sounding so picture perfect and memorable,

But once my heart feels connected like a lock in a key,

It'll hurt me to know I've so much to lose.

I appear and disappear in a blink of an eye,

Like a wandering gypsy by a sandy seashore,

Under the vast sky shared by the world full of goodbyes,

As footprints of memories are left behind in minds,

But it's alright because waves of time will wash them away.

Don't cry for me once I'm gone in the mist,

I never meant to stay in one place for a long play,

But I know you would still move on in bliss,

Like the pain deep inside, I'll be forgotten in a few days.

39. IRREPLACABLE VOID

Have you ever felt,

That one feeling devouring deep inside,

Filling up your chest with pain,

That keeps hurting on repeat as you've cried,

Begging the voices to stop inside your brain.

That stubborn void,

Leaving permanent marks on your heart,

As nothing can defeat it,

Nor the blood that rushed through your veins,

Can replace the emptiness.

You may run,

But there's no way you can hide,

As it tries to bottle up minds with wars,

And crushing dreams every single night,

But it's impossible to be truly happy like before,

Because of how much you've grown,

As well as the feelings that've hidden deep inside.

If they break apart,

So would you as the void is part of you.

40. SOMETHING MUST BE ......

Something must be wrong with me,
Addicted to keep all the hurt inside,
Always bursting with an enormous amount of anger,
But never once feeling any pride.
Something must be wrong with me
If all I do is stay silent and cry,
So clueless of how to stop the aching pain,
But all I want to do is run away or die.
Something must be wrong with me,
If I constantly allow my emotions to go wild,
Stuck in an endless loop of confusion,
Making me feel like a lost child.
Something must be wrong with me,
If I can't fight against the poisonous thoughts,
Forcing me to question my daily actions and mind,
Twisting my stomach into messy knots.
Something is truly wrong with me,
When I think there's only one way out,
Pouring the nightmares into the form of words,
With drenched eyes and a noisy mind as it shouts,
Begging helplessly for me to ease them.

41. DYSTOPIA

You've drained the color from my skies,
Blinded my youth with an ocean of lies,
But I don't know what is this new feeling,
Drowning in confusion as I ask myself;
If this is a true reality or if I'm daydreaming.
You've crushed my heart into million pieces,
Just like you're slowly damaging me inside,
Honestly,
I can't breathe,
You're suffocating me with chains of agony,
Surrounded by blurry messes as visions turn unclear.
Hear my soft cries and trembling voice,
Admire the tears flowing out of my reddened eyes,
To escape the hollow feeling and shadow's grip,
Clueless of where I'll run to with naked feet,
Dont come near,
You'll drag both of us down into a nightmare.
Because everytime I'm with you,
I'm in dystopia.

42. BUEATY HURTS

I was once obsessed in beauty,
Carelessly allowed my ears to catch words of hate,
So the burning urge of letting myself starve,
Slowly growing each day as I barely ate.
I can't help it but wanting more,
I suffered my body for others' satisfaction,
It was so for others to like me a little more,
Greedy for perfection and attentions.
But my friend once told me,
Wait a minute and stare at the mirror,
Look at what you've become,
Fatigued eyes, pale skin and a weak smile over your face.
Beauty hurts, she said.
Why would you put yourself through pain?
Just for slight happiness that you could possibly gain?
Was that really what you thought your life worth?
And why were you obsessed in beauty on the outside,
When all you've was an ugly heart on the inside?

43. PEAK OF MIND:FIRST SIDE

Here we have happiness,
The most sought out state of being.
It's usually drown itself into the music,
Be one with the slow beat and quiet rhythm,
As they makes you forget your mistakes,
Or the unfortunate day that faith has given.
You think of falling asleep in a lover's grip,
Or the favorite things that you've been craving,
Or an unexpected reply from close friends.
It's about spending time on your bed,
While the rain soothes you from outside,
It's beautiful how a mind works,
Full of pictures that you wish to come to life.

44. PEAK OF MIND: OTHER SIDE

On this side we have sadness,
Because it feels like you've lost someone,
Despite that it's barely even true at all.
It's usually the one that drowns you deep,
As an invisible weight rushes in like water,
Making you suffocate due to the lack of air,
As you beg for life to treat you better.
You think of falling down into an endless abyss,
Or the possibility of what people think of you,
Or an unwanted comment from a passerby.
It's about spending time on your bed,
While having a silent war with your head,
It's dangerous how a mind works,
Full of pictures that makes you want to disappear.

www.ingramcontent.com/pod-product-compliance
Lightning Source LLC
Chambersburg PA
CBHW020648160726
47991CB00003B/1087